HOT SHOTS AND
HIGH SPOTS

GEORGE NAPOLITANO'S AMAZING PICTORIAL
HISTORY OF WRESTLING'S GREATEST STARS

HOT SHOTS AND HIGH SPOTS

GEORGE NAPOLITANO'S AMAZING PICTORIAL
HISTORY OF WRESTLING'S GREATEST STARS

ECW Press

Published by ECW Press
2120 Queen Street East, Suite 200, Toronto, Ontario, Canada M4E 1E2
416-694-3348 / info@ecwpress.com

Library and Archives Canada Cataloguing in Publication

Napolitano, George
Hot shots and high spots : George Napolitano's amazing pictorial history of wrestling's greatest stars / George Napolitano.

ISBN 978-1-55022-996-7
Also issued as
978-1-77090-064-6 (EPUB); 978-1-77090-065-3 (PDF)

1. Wrestling—History. 2. Wrestling—Pictorial works. 3. Wrestlers—Biography. I. Title.

GV1195.N36 2011   796.812022'2   C2011-902842-5

Editor: Michael Holmes
Cover and text layout and design: Cyanotype
Printing: Courier   1   2   3   4   5

Printed and bound in the United States

ECW PRESS
ecwpress.com

DEDICATION

This book is dedicated to my wife, Jackie, and my sons, Gregory and Joseph, who put up with all my travels through the years, as well as my granddaughters, Zoe and Ella.

In 1971 "Gentleman" Jim Valiant took on the Grand Wizard as his manager and changed his moniker to "Handsome" Jimmy Valiant. Incidentally, The Grand Wizard was the person who talked to Mr. Vince McMahon Sr. on my behalf. It was through his help that I was able to get a foothold in the wrestling world.

I became addicted to professional wrestling in the early '60s. Growing up in Brooklyn, New York, you could watch it three nights a week on channel five. Tuesday's matches were broadcast from Sunnyside Gardens in Queens. On Wednesday they came from the Bridgeport Arena in Bridgeport, Connecticut. Thursday's action came from the Capital Centre in Washington, D.C.

My heroes at the time were Bruno Sammartino, "Cowboy" Bob Ellis and the Bastien Brothers. As far as I was concerned they could do no wrong. The champion was "Nature Boy" Buddy Rogers, and no matter who he faced, he would always find a way to win — despite the best efforts of men like Dory Dixon, Bearcat Wright, and Johnny Valentine. It wasn't until May 17, 1963, that Buddy Rogers finally met defeat — and in a mere 47 seconds no less — to my hero, Bruno Sammartino, in Madison Square Garden. What made it even more special was that I was there in person, sitting in the balcony watching as Bruno was crowned the new champion of the world.

After Sammartino's victory I continued to watch wrestling and root on my favorites, but as 1964 rolled in and a group of "lads from Liverpool" known as the Beatles took the world by storm, my interest changed from wrestling to music and girls. Like so many boys my age I picked up the guitar, learned how to play, and started a band, called the Creations, with my childhood friends. Soon we were practicing every night, and eventually playing every weekend. There was no time to watch wrestling, or any other sport for that matter. In 1965 the Creations became a local Brooklyn favorite, and Mercury Records eventually signed us to a recording contract. For a variety of reasons we didn't release our first record until 1968, when we were known as the Ox-Bow Incident. We went on to release three 45s, none of which became hits — though all are hanging on my wall. It was an experience I will never forget.

Around this time I was fortunate to get a Nikon camera and I began photographing the band and the various people and places we'd encounter on our travels. In June of 1970 while reading the *New York Daily News*, I noticed an ad for a wrestling show at Madison Square Garden. I asked Jackie, my girlfriend at the time (we were later married and have been happy for 40 years), if she wanted to go. I hadn't watched wrestling in years, and she had *never* watched a match on TV or in person. She readily agreed, saying it would be a fun thing to do. On July 10, 1970, we watched Chief Jay Strongbow, Victor Rivera, Mario Milano and my all-time childhood favorite, Bruno Sammartino (who was wrestling Crusher Verdu). We sat in Section 108 in the Loge and during the matches I would run down the aisle with my trusty Nikon in hand, trying to take photographs.

During the evening the MC announced that there was going to be another card the following Saturday afternoon at Sunnyside Garden in Queens. When Saturday came we went to Sunnyside to see the action up close and personal. Once again I took my camera, and during the matches I ran down the aisle to try to get a better shot. At some point, a man sitting ringside said, "You must be getting great pictures; you have a great camera." When the matches were over the gentleman introduced himself as J.F. Sanchez-Acosta and said that he worked for *Ring* magazine. He told me that if I ever came back to Sunnyside Gardens to bring some photos with me. Needless to say we went again the following month, and I brought some of the pictures I took. The man looked at the photos and must have liked what he saw, because he asked me if I wanted to work for *Ring* magazine.

I had no idea what I was getting myself into!

The following month I arrived at Sunnyside Gardens early in the afternoon and met Mr. Sanchez-Acosta. He immediately brought me downstairs to the dressing room where I was introduced to Arnold Skaaland. Mr. Sanchez-Acosta told Mr. Skaaland that I was going to be his ringside photographer. Mr. Skaaland put out his hand and shook mine and told me to have a good time, but to be careful to stay out of the way of the wrestlers.

That day I met "Gentleman" Jim Valiant in the dressing room, and he was the first wrestler I officially photographed. After the matches were over I interviewed Valiant, and a month or so later I had my first story published in *Ring Wrestling*. In April 2011, some 40 years after our first introduction, I saw Jimmy Valiant at the Cauliflower Alley Club dinner in Las Vegas, Nevada, and we reminiscenced about the "old" days. Who would have imagined that we would be standing together so many years later after that chance meeting in a cramped dressing room? That day in Sunnyside Gardens was the start of an adventure of 40-plus years that has taken me to practically every state in the U.S., as well as all around the world to such exotic locations as Germany, Austria, Mexico, Puerto Rico, Aruba, Curaçao, Trinidad and Japan.

My first job in the sport was writing stories and taking photos for *Ring Wrestling*. I later became a contributor for *Wrestling Revue* and *Wrestling Monthly* magazines as well as a contributor to *Wrestling World* magazine, *The Big Book of Wrestling* and numerous other titles. In the mid-'70s I became editor and photographer for the WWWF programs, editor of the East Coast edition of *Wrestling News* and later editor of the *WWWF Wrestling Action* magazine that was advertised on the WWWF wrestling television program.

In 1981 I became editor of *Wrestling's Main Event* magazine, and a couple of years later edited the series of magazines published by Starlog including *Wrestling Scene*, *Ringside Wrestling*, *Wrestling All Stars*, *Superstar Wrestler*, *Wrestling Reporter*, *Bad Ass Dudes*, *Beauties of Wrestling* and countless other titles. My association with Starlog Publications lasted nearly 20 years, but by 2000, with the advent of the Internet and rising cost for everything associated with the magazine industry, Starlog was sold and ceased publication.

Through the years I have also written 11 coffee table books that were well received by the wrestling community: *The Pictorial History of Wrestling: The Good, The Bad and The Ugly*, *Great Grudge Matches*, *The All-Star Wrestling Postcard Book*, *The Complete Book of Wrestling*, *This Is Wrestling!*, *The New Pictorial History of Wrestling*, *Wrestling Bashers and Beauties*, *Wrestling Heroes & Villains*, *The Mighty Maulers*, *Wrestling: The Greatest Stars* and *Championship Wrestling*.

During my 40-plus years photographing and reporting I have witnessed the wrestling landscape change from one where regional territories existed throughout the U.S. to a place where the WWE and TNA are the main forces in the industry. I have seen thousands and thousands of wrestlers ply their craft and watched an infinite number of matches, but a few stand out.

I was fortunate to be on the field at Shea Stadium on September 30, 1972, for the Bruno Sammartino–Pedro Morales match that ended in a draw after 1 hour and 15 minutes. That was the first big card I covered, and fortunately it wasn't the last. I was back at Shea Stadium again on June 25, 1976, when Bruno Sammartino exacted revenge on Stan Hansen for his neck injury suffered in Madison Square Garden. (A side note to this: Mr. Vince McMahon Sr. asked me if I would drive Stan Hansen out of the Garden and back to the Howard Johnson Hotel after the incident with Sammartino. Fortunately for us we were able to get out of the Garden alive.) Also on the Shea Stadium card was the closed circuit match between Muhammed Ali and Antonio Inoki from Tokyo, Japan. On August 9, 1980, the WWF returned to Shea Stadium with a card headlined by a steel cage match between Bruno Sammartino and as his former pupil Larry Zbyszko. This show also featured a bout between Andre the Giant and Hulk Hogan. Andre was victorious in this battle of Titans when he pinned Hogan in 7:48.

Looking back I realize that I was at nearly every major show and pay-per-view that took place in the '80s and '90s. I attended the first Starrcade in Greensboro, North Carolina, as well as every other NWA Starrcade event; numerous Halloween Havoc, Super Clash, Super Brawl and Crocket Cup battles; the Great American Bash; Bash at the Beach;

the AWA "Wrestle-Rock" extravaganza at the Metrodome in Minneapolis; major events at Municipal Stadium in Cleveland, Comiskey Park in Chicago, the Superdome in New Orleans, Texas Stadium; and countless other cards big and small in bingo halls, church auditoriums, roller rinks and outdoor stadiums all over the U.S. and throughout the world. Not to mention, I have attended every WrestleMania, SummerSlam, Survivor Series and Royal Rumble card. To say that I have seen it all would be an understatement; but truth be told, unlike many wrestling fanatics, I really cannot name the matches on any particular card or event — there have simply been too many to remember.

I would have to say that, to me, the '90s were the most exciting time in wrestling. Whether it was WCW, ECW or the WWF, every week there was a major event taking place somewhere. During this era I was pumping out four, five or six newsstand magazines a month and I was always on the go. While there were quite a few stars in this decade, my favorites were the nWo group lead by Scott Hall, Kevin Nash, X-Pac and "Hollywood" Hulk Hogan, as well as the WWF twosome of "Stone Cold" Steve Austin and the Rock. The nWo completely changed the face of wrestling. Because of them it was cool to be bad, and this extended over into the WWE with "Stone Cold" Steve Austin and the Rock. With the WCW–WWF Monday night ratings war in full swing you just never knew what was going to happen on any given night.

The '90s was also the era for my favorite promotion of all time, ECW. While the original Extreme Championship Wrestling existed only from 1992 to 2001, the impact it had on the sport can still be felt today. Fans still cheer, "E-C-W!" whenever anyone performs a death-defying move. With stars such as Cactus Jack, Sabu, Shane Douglas, Rob Van Dam, Tommy Dreamer, Taz, Terry Funk and the Dudleys, ECW became the "in" promotion. For those who may not realize it, ECW borrowed heavily from old-school Texas brawling and combined this with the type of matches that I was fortunate to attend and photograph in Puerto Rico and Japan's FMW. With this wild and crazy hybrid style, ECW grew from a small outlaw regional promotion based in Philadelphia, to one that, at its height, nearly rivaled WCW and the WWF in popularity.

This book would not have been possible without the help and cooperation of the thousands and thousands of professional wrestlers and current sports-entertainers that I have met and become friends with throughout the years. I also have to publicly thank the promoters throughout the country that put together the shows in venues large and small where I have covered this amazing sport. I would be remiss if I did not thank the original WWWF/WWF CEO, Mr. Vince McMahon Sr., and his son, Vincent K. McMahon, and his family, for allowing me to become a part of their wrestling family all these years. I would also have to thank my wife, Jackie, and my sons, Gregory and Joseph, for putting up with my wrestling addiction for all these years and allowing me to bring many of the stars into our home.

The photos in this book are a collection of many of my favorites. Not all of them are action packed, nor are they technically the "best" photographs in the purest sense of the word, but each has a special meaning to me and tells part of the story of my years covering this amazing, exciting hybrid now called sports-entertainment. I hope you enjoy the retrospective.

— *George Napolitano*

Taz suplexes Bam Bam Bigelow.

"The Giant" Paul Wight, before his days as "The Big Show," tossing Rey Mysterio into the stands during a WCW match.

Rick Steiner was one of those quiet guys who would do anything for you. Once I mentioned to him that my son Gregory wrestled on his Xaverian High School wrestling team. Rick, who was a sensational collegiate wrestler, made it his business to come to one of Gregory's wrestling practices the next time he was in New York.

Bubba Ray Dudley, along with "brother" Devon, became breakout stars in ECW. Prior to his ECW stint, Bubba bounced around for several years in independent promotions in New York trying to get a break. I first met Bubba Ray in 1992 at Kuschers Country Club in upstate New York when he worked for Mario Savoldi's IWCCW promotion, and we have remained close ever since.

Jesse Neal is on the receiving end of a vicious 3D delivered courtesy of the Dudley Boys during a show in MCU Park in Brooklyn.

Stone Cold stuns "Rowdy" Roddy Piper during a segment of "Piper's Pit."

The Deadman and the Rock. The Undertaker could have been a star in any era. From his eerie ring entrance to the moment when he delivers his Tombstone pile driver and pins his hapless opponent, everyone's eyes are riveted on him. He was by far the most exciting wrestler in the sport during the '90s and continues to be a WWE mainstay today.

Abyss attempts to twist Jeff Hardy's head off his shoulders.

Terry Funk in ECW.

Rob Van Dam goes skyward as he delivers his devastating Five-Star Frog Splash to A.J. Styles.

"Stone Cold" Steve Austin and his arch nemesis the "Evil" Mr. McMahon propelled the WWF back into the mainstream again.

Dancing with the Stars contestant and rock 'n' roll singer Chris Jericho displays one of his many championship belts during his wrestling days.

"The Outsiders" X-Pac, Scott Hall and Kevin Nash were the talk of the wrestling scene in 1997. After coming from the WWF, the Outsiders literally took over WCW, and in a few short months had the wrestling world abuzz with their wild and crazy antics. In 1997 and '98 due to the popularity (or unpopularity) of the nWo, WCW became the show to watch on Monday nights.

Terry and Dory Funk are the only brothers to each win the NWA World Heavyweight Championship. I first meet Terry in 1972 when he wrestled in Madison Square Garden with his dad, Dory Funk Sr. At the time the exploits of his brother Dory Jr. were well documented, but no one knew that Terry would become such an icon.

The Rock.

Sable turned quite a few heads during the 1997 Slammys. Her outfit at the black tie affair left little to the imagination.

"Classy" Freddie Blassie and Nikolai Volkoff give me a wrestling lesson.

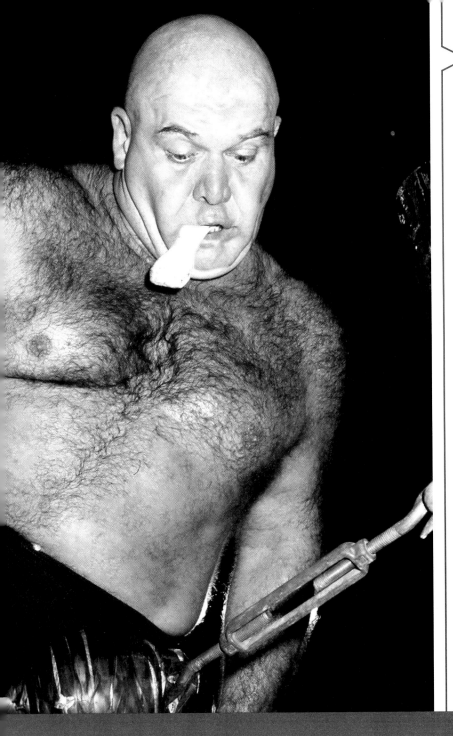

The original Animal: George Steele.
He was in a class by himself!

Triple H and Vince McMahon.

Mr. Fuji shows off his karate skills as he breaks a board held by his partner Professor Tanaka. WWWF announcer Vince McMahon Jr. announces the action during a televised interview from the Philadelphia Arena in 1976.

Mil Máscaras and Bruno Sammartino were two of the most conditioned athletes during the '70s. At that time the wrestlers as a whole were not known for their physical prowess but more for their physical makeup. The exceptions to this were Sammartino, Máscaras, "Superstar" Billy Graham, Rocky Johnson and Tony Atlas.

Randy Orton in 2002.

I first met Triple H in 1993 at a small show in Connecticut that was run by legendary wrestler Killer Kowalski. Triple H's name at that time was Terra Ryzing, and with his colorful robe and long blond hair he reminded me of a young Ric Flair. Watching him in action you could just sense that he had that special something that could propel him to stardom. After our formal introduction by Killer Kowalski I took several photos of him, and he thanked me for taking the time to photograph him. I published the photos in my *Wrestling All Stars* magazine and several months later, while photographing the matches in WCW, I felt a tap on my shoulder and saw a hand reach out. It was Triple H. This time he was known as Jean-Paul

The young Hunter Hearst Helmsley.

Lévesque and he immediately thanked me for publishing the photos that I took of him in Connecticut. Having met him in his formative stage I looked upon him with interest and kept tabs on his progress.

In 1995 he joined the WWF and Hunter Hearst Helmsley was born. Through hard work and perseverance Triple H has made himself into one of the top performers in the world. Along the way he earned 23 championships in the WWE and married Stephanie McMahon. Together they have three beautiful children. Through all his success Triple H has remained the same likeable person that I first met in a small high school gym in Connecticut when he was trying to climb the ladder of success.

Chavo and Hector Guerrero taught their younger brother Eddie the ins and outs of the business.

In 1972 when I worked for *Wrestling Revue* magazine, also on the staff was an up-and-coming wrestler who had yet to become a "king" named Jerry Lawler. Every month Jerry would contribute a comic strip of a wrestler he called "The Patriot." Maybe someday the Patriot will come to life on a WWE telecast.

Dwayne "The Rock" Johnson's wrestling career spanned from 1996 to 2004, and while his tenure was short when compared to those of other wrestlers, he left a lasting legacy in the WWF. The Rock joined the WWF during their "war" with WCW, and while he wasn't one of the more popular wrestlers during those first few years when he wrestled as Rocky Maivia, his popularity eventually increased due in part to his feud with Mr. McMahon, his love-hate relationship with "Stone Cold" Steve Austin, his catchphrases and his exceptional microphone skills. In March 2011 the Rock finally returned to the WWE to be the guest host for *WrestleMania XXVII*. When the main event between the Miz and John Cena ended in a draw, the Rock ran to ringside and ordered that the match be restarted. No sooner had the match resumed than the Rock hit Cena with his Rock Bottom. As soon as Cena hit the mat, the Miz covered him to win the match. The following night on Raw, Cena called the Rock out for interfering in his bout, and the two wrestlers agreed to wrestle against each other at *Wrestle-Mania XXVIII* in Miami. With this return, the Rock may extend his wrestling tenure after all.

Rocky Johnson was an exceptional scientific wrestler in his day and captured numerous titles all over the world.

Batista brutalizing former Evolution stablemate Triple H during a match at *WrestleMania 21*.

Before making it big in the WWE, Steve Austin wrestled in WCW with Lady Blossom by his side.

The Fabulous Freebirds — Michael Hayes , Terry Gordy and Buddy Roberts from Bad Street, USA — were the toast of the town in 1985. This photo was taken at the record release party for Michael Hayes' single "Badstreet USA" in Dallas, Texas.

The Game.

Early Hulk: a heel with a mouthpiece.

Koko B. Ware and Frankie. They were quite a hit during the early *WrestleMania* era.

"Stone Cold" Steve Austin celebrates as only he knows how.

Rob Van Dam: Mr. Monday Night, or "The Whole F'N Show" — he never fails to excite.

Two great Italian athletes, Bruno Sammartino and Joe DiMaggio, meet face to face in Atlantic City on October 23, 1982, for a "Greatest Sports Legends" 10th anniversary reunion event at Bally's. When I showed Bruno this photo years later, he was flabbergasted and wanted a copy for his collection.

This is the first photo taken of Randy Savage in the WWWF. I took it before a TV taping in Philadelphia. At the time, he went by his given name: Randy Poffo.

Mr. Vince McMahon Sr. gets together with High Chief Peter Maivia in the dressing room at Madison Square Garden. Mr. McMahon Sr. was a special person, a kind and gentle man. I will always be indebted to him for allowing me access to his promotion and for making my job so much easier.

Greg "The Hammer" Valentine puts Tony Atlas into a Boston Crab in one of his early bouts in the WWF. I first met Valentine in 1973 when he wrestled as Johnny Fargo in the National Wrestling Federation. Early in his career his dad, Johnny Valentine, didn't want Greg to use the family name because the senior Valentine didn't want to appear too old to still be wrestling. The younger Valentine first adopted the name Johnny Valentine Jr., but settled upon Greg Valentine, and was billed as Johnny Valentine's brother. It wasn't until 1976 when he joined the NWA and began to wrestle for Mid-Atlantic Championship Wrestling that it was revealed that he was the son of the great Johnny Valentine. Greg made his first appearance in the WWWF in 1978 and we became fast friends traveling together whenever we could.

Vince McMahon is all smiles as he carries the World Championship belt on his shoulder. Mr. Vince McMahon, the current WWE Chairman and CEO, took a regional wrestling promotion and made it into a huge conglomerate incorporating television shows and movies. Along the way he has entertained countless millions week after week, year after year, with first-run live television programs from around the world. I have known Mr. McMahon since 1971 and he has always been very respectful and cordial to me and my family. If it weren't for his help and guidance, I would not have been able to perform the job I love for all these years.

Oh Yeah! "The Macho Man" Randy Savage was another wrestler I watched work very hard to get to the top. I first met Randy Savage, who was then known as Randy Poffo, backstage at the Philadelphia Arena in 1974. Poffo was a minor league baseball player at the time, and he was brought to Philadelphia by "The Grand Wizard" Ernie Roth to wrestle on the WWWF TV tapings as a favor to Randy's dad, Angelo Poffo. The Wiz asked me to take a photo of Poffo and told me that someday this kid could be something. At the time he didn't look the part, but when the Wizard asks you to do something, you do it. Through the years we kept in touch and from time to time, he'd send photos and clippings of his escapades in Kentucky to use in the magazines. Then one day out of the blue I saw "Macho Man" Randy Savage on the WWF telecast, and he looked phenomenal. With his valet Miss Elizabeth by his side, the two were a perfect fit for the WWF. Savage made his mark in the WWF, and then like many others reinvented himself in WCW, where his career continued to grow.

High Chief Peter Maivia, the Rock's grandfather.

Tito Santana during his days as Intercontinental Champion.

When Kurt Angle first broke into the business, a Japanese magazine requested that I go to a spot show in New Jersey to photograph him because he was going to be a future champion. Obviously they knew what they were talking about.

Superstar Billy Graham battles Bruno Sammartino. The two archenemies had many battles leading up to their April 30, 1977, bout in Baltimore when the Superstar finally won the WWWF world heavyweight title. Fortunately I was there to witness the battle.

I visited Andre in the hospital after his match with Killer Khan. The cast they put on Andre's leg was the biggest that hospital had ever made.

Out of the thousands and thousands of photographs that I have taken, this is by far my most famous. The photo was taken outside the dressing room at the Philadelphia Arena in 1972 and was used as a publicity shot wherever Andre would appear.

When I saw Joyce Grable at the Cauliflower Alley Club convention in Las Vegas in April 2011, the first thing she did was mention it to me. Then she said, "I wanted to be in that photo so bad. I was a little late coming out of my dressing room and Vicki Williams took my spot. I've heard some people say that Andre wasn't holding the girls up and the photo was a fake. But I was there and I should know. In the photo, with Williams, are Daisy Mae, Donna Christanello and Debbie Johnson. Vince McMahon Sr. himself asked us to take the photo with Andre and we were thrilled to do it. We saw copies of that photo everywhere we went."

While Andre's appetite was legendary, no one could keep pace with his drinking. I remember seeing Andre chug-a-lugging a bottle of Rémy Martin as he sat in the back during one of those long bus trips in Japan.

Rob Van Dam and A.J. Styles go at it fiercely during their battle.

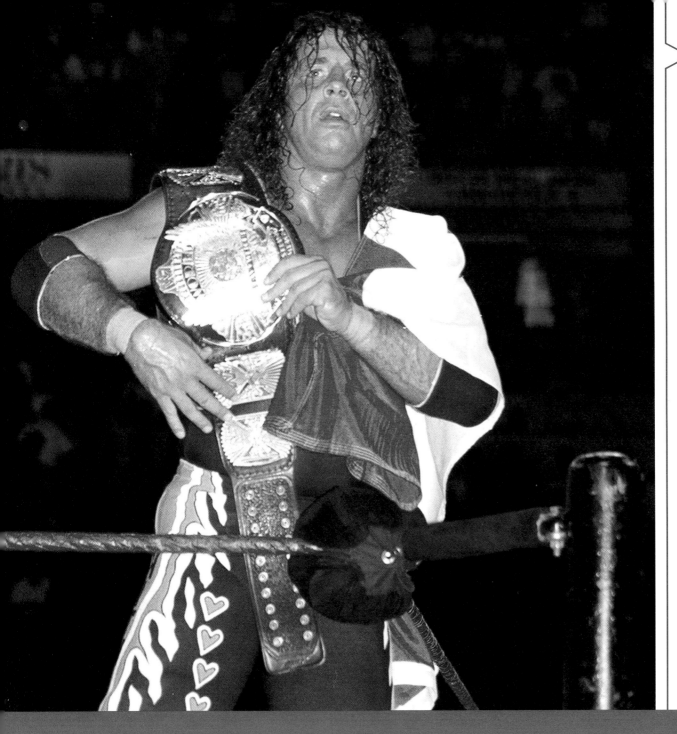

To many in the wrestling industry, Bret "The Hitman" Hart was the best wrestler of all time.

WWE's new breed: John Cena and "The Animal" Batista celebrate with their respective titles early in their careers.

The young rocker: Shawn Michaels.

The Greatest and the Hulkster.

The Rock.

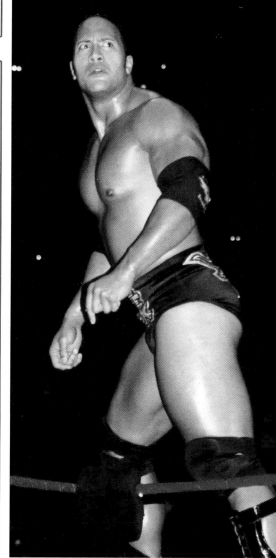

Mil Máscaras checks out the biceps of "Mr. USA" Tony Atlas.

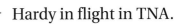
Hardy in flight in TNA.

This photo was used many places to show how wide Andre the Giant's arm span was. To Andre's left are Chief Jay Strongbow and Mike Pappas, and to his right is Victor Rivera.

The Ultimate Warrior with the WWF title.

He may be the littlest man in a big man's sport, but no one has as much heart and desire as Rey Mysterio. What I saw in Mil Máscaras in the '70s, Rey Mysterio has perfected and brought to the new generation.

Today's biggest star John Cena basks in the cheers of the crowd.

Andre the Giant meets Muhammad Ali during a press conference in 1976 to announce the Shea Stadium bout between Andre and Chuck Wepner, and the Tokyo "Wrestler vs. Boxer" battle between Ali and Antonio Inoki.

Mil Máscaras was my favorite wrestler to photograph in the '70s. He was colorful and did so much more than most of the other wrestlers of that era. Máscaras' high-flying antics paved the way for stars such as Rey Misterio, Sin Cara, and Máscaras' nephew, Alberto Del Rio.

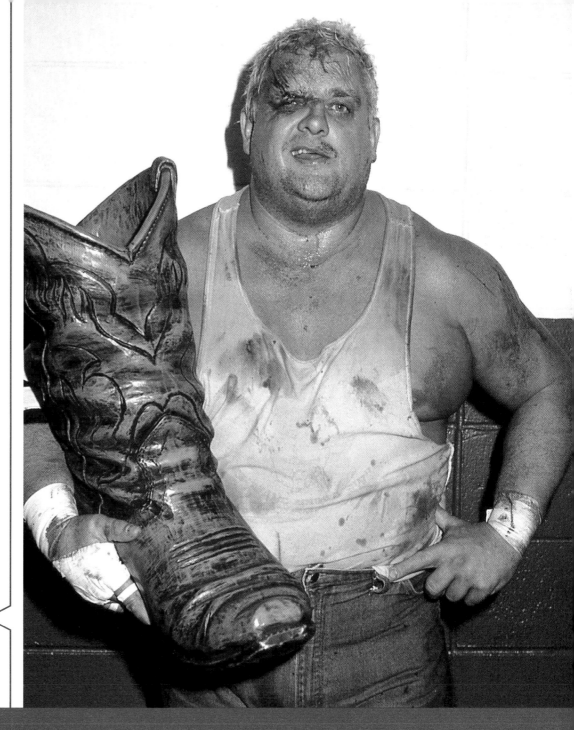

Dusty Rhodes, the American Dream.

What can I say that hasn't been said a thousand times before? Ric Flair is undoubtedly the greatest wrestler that I have ever seen. He began his career in 1972, and he's still going at it in 2011. That's nearly 40 years of mat action. In fact, Ric Flair has been wrestling nearly as long as I have been taking wrestling photographs. (Having started in 1970, I actually have him beat by two years, but who's counting?) Through the years I have been fortunate to be with Ric all over the U.S. as well as in Puerto Rico and the Dominican Republic, and every time it was an adventure. Unfortunately many of the stories can't be published, but whatever you may have heard . . . is all true. Trust me! During his heyday Flair not only was the best in-ring technician, he also was the best showman. There have been many great wrestlers through the years, but when you talk about the complete package, no one can match up to "Nature Boy" Ric Flair.

"The Nature Boy" Ric Flair.

Harley Race grimaces as Flair delivers one of his patented chops: Woooooooooooo!

Ricky "The Dragon" Steamboat was the best pure scientific wrestler that I ever saw. He could do it all. His matches with "Nature Boy" Ric Flair were always ring classics.

Flair had one of the great ring entrances of all time. But in haste to get to the ring before this match he forgot to remove his Rolex — he slipped it to me at ringside to hold until the bout was through.

Kevin Von Erich clamps his sleeper hold on Ric Flair during the Heaven Needed a Champion card at Texas Stadium.

"I'm a limousine ridin', jet flyin', kiss stealin', wheelin' dealin' son of a gun. Wooo!"

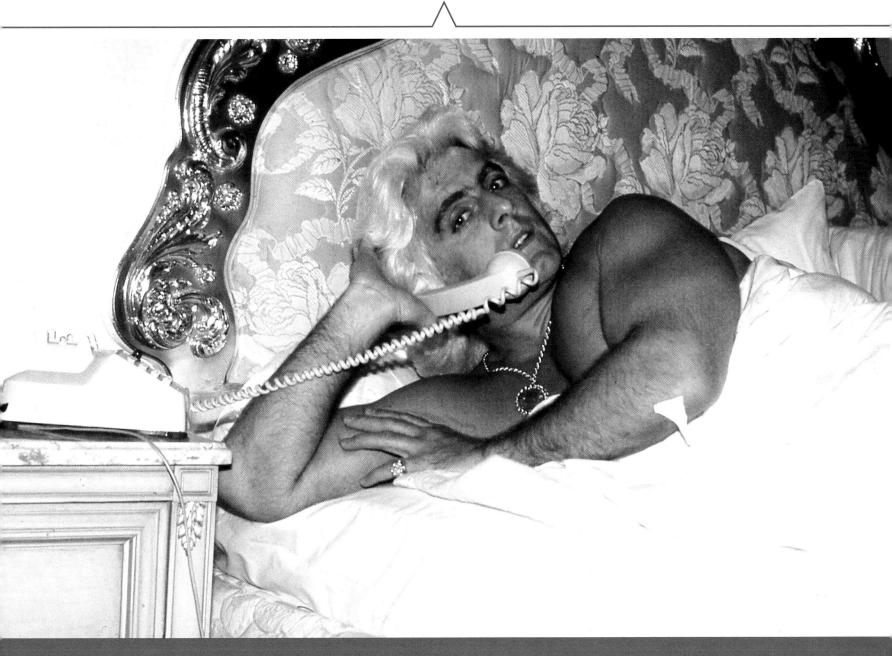

The Honky Tonk Man checks out a guitar to use on one of his unsuspecting opponents in John Castellano's Guitar City store in Brooklyn, New York.

In a match in San Juan, Puerto Rico, Abdullah the Butcher uses his trusty fork on Tony Atlas. I first met Abdullah in 1972 when he wrestled for the National Wrestling Federation in upstate New York. I later met him again in Montreal at Jarry Park, and in subsequent years I have seen him wrestle all around the world. Of these many encounters, one vividly stands out in my mind. In 1988 in Trinidad, we got into a cab after the matches to ride back to our hotel. I was seated next to the driver, with Abdullah next to me, and crammed in the back seat were Mr. Fuji, Gama Singh and Bobby Jaggers. As the taxi driver started to pull out of his parking spot, his path was blocked by hundreds of fans pounding on his cab. The driver jumped out of his cab and started to argue with the fans, pleading with them to stop banging on the car. The fans became even more unruly and began to rock the car. Fuji, Gama Singh and Abdullah started to get a little more concerned until Abdullah pushed me behind the wheel and said, "Get us out of here." Using driving techniques I learned dodging cabs on the streets of New York City, I managed to break away from the crowd, and as I did I could see the taxi driver running after the cab. I drove

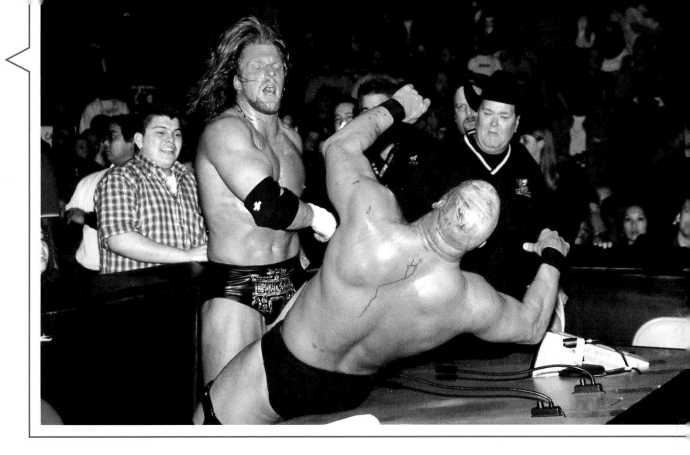

Triple H battles Stone Cold in front of Jim Ross.

the cab to our hotel, and we jumped out of the car and went to our rooms. A short while later I heard a knock on the door: it was the police. They were looking for me for stealing the cab! I was taken to the lobby and luckily Abdullah was sitting there trying to get something to eat. When he saw the commotion, he came over and explained to the police officers what had happened. They weren't too pleased with the story, but after a while, thanks to Abdullah's insistence, they let me go.

In retrospect, out of the thousands of wrestlers that I have photographed over the course of my 40-plus years in this sport, I have known Abdullah the longest. That's why it was a thrill for me to see him get inducted into the Wrestling Hall of Fame in his hometown of Atlanta, Georgia, in 2011. After all these years it was great to see Abdullah the Butcher get the recognition he so richly deserved.

"King Kong" Bundy appears to be squeezing the life out of Brutus "The Barber" Beefcake.

Jerry "The King" Lawler holds up both the AWA title and the WCCW world championship belt after defeating Kerry Von Erich in Chicago on December 13, 1988.

Mikey Whipwreck gets a lift, compliments of Bam Bam Bigelow.

The devilish Kevin Sullivan.

The Stinger and the Nature Boy.

While Hulk Hogan is generally regarded as the man who gave the WWF its mainstream popularity with the first *WrestleMania*, the truth of the matter is that without an able opponent like "Rowdy" Roddy Piper, the WWE might not still be doing worldwide business. Piper and Paul Orndorff were Hulk Hogan and Mr. T.'s opponents in the first *WrestleMania* at Madison Square Garden, and their careers continued to be intertwined in the ensuing years.

My first encounter with Roddy Piper came in San Antonio, Texas, in 1974 when he was the Americas Champion. I didn't see him again until 1981 when Greg Valentine drove me from Richmond, Virginia, to Charlotte, North Carolina. During the drive Greg told me that he had a room for me in Charlotte. He failed to mention that the room was in his friend's apartment. Little did I know that his friend was Roddy Piper. At 4 a.m. we arrived in Charlotte, and Greg, as only he could, knocked on

Kamala "The Ugandan Giant" in full regalia during a photo shoot for one of my books.

his friend's door waking him from a sound sleep. Greg proceeded to tell him that I was his friend from New York and that I needed a place to stay for the night. Roddy said of course, and took out sheets, pillows and a blanket and made up the bed for me. He told me that there was food and drinks in the fridge and to make myself at home. We have remained friends ever since.

Jimmy "Superfly" Snuka was far and away the most colorful wrestler that I saw in the '70s-era WWWF. Whether alone or with "Captain" Lou Albano by his side, the Superfly did it all.

The Iron Sheik locks his camel clutch on Sgt. Slaughter. The Iron Sheik and Sgt. Slaughter battled numerous times in the WWF and the AWA, and each battle was a classic.

Scott Steiner was one of the best pure scientific wrestlers in the sport. He learned his craft while wrestling in college and became a standout in WCW.

Randy Orton was still a green rookie when I first encountered him in Atlantic City in 2002. Being a third generation wrestler, with his dad, Bob, and grandfather Bob Orton Sr. having been such big stars in the sport, I knew that he was a man who bore watching. Needless to say Rany Orton has more than lived up to expectations and will only get better and better as the years go by.

Sting: 1999.

The original Sheik was hardcore before the word was invented. Throughout the '70s I would often go to Detroit's Cobo Hall to see the Sheik in action. But whenever you went to Cobo you had to shoot fast and often because the Sheik rarely spent much time inside the ring. The wildest I ever saw Sheik was in his Texas Death chair match with Tex McKenzie. Chairs were legal and both men pounded each other senseless. But my favorite Sheik match occurred in the Boston Gardens, when the wild man took on then-WWWF champion Pedro Morales. His long time manager Abdullah Farouk, who was better known to WWWF fans as "The Grand Wizard," accompanied the Sheik to the ring and it was bedlam from the start.

The Macho Man.

Superstar Billy Graham.

Back in the day no one would have ever predicted that Jesse "The Body" Ventura would someday become Governor of Minnesota.

Triple H and the classic ring entrance.

"Classy" Freddie Blassie holds up my son Gregory as comedian and wrestling fan Andy Kaufman stands by before a match in Madison Square Garden.

Kurt Angle suplexes Randy Orton from the second rope during a match early in their respective careers.

King Kong Bundy faced Hulk Hogan in *WrestleMania 2* in Los Angeles and nearly crushed the mighty Hulkster to death.

Carlos Colón battles Hercules Ayala in a barbed wire fire match in Bayamón, Puerto Rico. This was by far the most dangerous match that I ever covered, as the flames continually blew in my direction whenever the air-conditioning went on. In fact I remember getting singed by the flames as I tried to get a closer shot of the action.

Before Cyndi Lauper came around with the Rock 'n' Wrestling connection, Debbie Harry from Blondie was a fixture at Madison Square Garden events in the '70s, and "Captain" Lou Albano was one of her favorites.

High-flying Jeff Hardy lands his Swanton onto the fallen Abyss in Brooklyn.

Mick Foley made his wrestling dream come true when he became Dude Love. While in high school, Foley invented the Dude Love character, and years later he actually had a chance to relive his dream in the WWF as Dude Love.

The Dudley Boys 3D Taz during their ECW encounter.

D-Generation X: Billy Gunn, X-Pac, Triple H, Chyna and "Road Dogg" Jesse James were quite a sensation in WWF.

J.J. Dillon leads the Four Horseman — Lex Luger, Tully Blanchard, Ric Flair and Arn Anderson — during their NWA days.

The governor and the chairman: Arnold Schwarzenegger and Vince McMahon got together in Baltimore in 1999.

"Rowdy" Roddy Piper brutalizes Greg "The Hammer" Valentine in this classic dog-collar confrontation.

On June 2, 1976, the great Muhammad Ali was at the Philadelphia Arena to promote his upcoming match with Antonio Inoki in Tokyo, Japan. When Ali jumped into the ring and challenged anyone to come and face him, Gorilla Monsoon took him up on his offer. After squaring off, Monsoon immediately picked up Ali, put him into his airplane spin and then dumped the Great One to the mat.

Afterwards I drove to the AP office in New York City and gave them the photo. AP put it on the wire, and the next day the photo was on the back page of newspapers across the country. Afterwards Mr. McMahon and the promoters behind the Ali–Inoki event couldn't thank me enough for making a wrestling event "mainstream."

The Hulkster with the nWo-ed WCW title.

The Rock and Wrestling Connection: Cyndi Lauper, "Captain" Lou Albano and Hulk Hogan. I introduced Cyndi Lauper and her then-manager David Wolfe to Albano in the lobby of the Howard Johnson Hotel in New York City. Being a huge wrestling fan, Cyndi wanted to cast Albano in the video for her song "Girls Just Want to Have Fun." I guess it worked out well for all of them.

"Big Sexy" Kevin Nash was one of the best in his heyday.

Mankind takes "Mr. Socko" out to play.

Bill Goldberg and Hulk Hogan made an interesting pair in 1998.

Kurt Angle bends Shawn Michaels' neck during one of their many brawls.

Kurt Angle catches Shawn Michaels in his patented ankle lock.

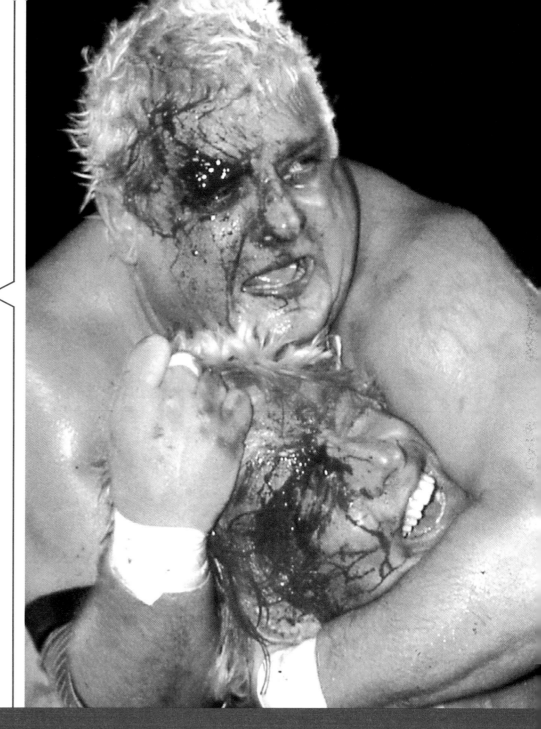

In his day there wasn't anyone more electrifying than "The American Dream" Dusty Rhodes. With his sing-song interviews and his crazy funky moves, Dusty Rhodes was the most colorful wrestler of his era. You could expect to see nothing but action whenever Dusty Rhodes was in the ring. Countless times I traveled to Florida to see Dusty Rhodes in action and he never disappointed. Whether he was battling Kevin Sullivan, the Purple Haze, Tully Blanchard or Ric Flair, you knew that you were going to be in for a treat.

Andy Kaufman, the self-proclaimed "Intergender Champion," gets together with Sherri Martel, Freddy Blassie and the Fabulous Moolah in the dressing room at Madison Square Garden. Kaufman is wearing a brace around his neck to alleviate the pain he suffered at the hands of Jerry Lawler during their match in Nashville.

Shawn Michaels, Triple H, Mike Tyson and Steve Austin behind the scenes.

Tiger Mask was a huge sensation in Japan. Satoru Sayama portrayed the original Tiger Mask in Japan, and he was an exceptional wrestler. I had the pleasure of seeing him in action in 1981 when I toured New Japan Pro Wrestling, and I was instantly impressed with his in-ring skills. At that time there really wasn't a viable Junior Heavyweight Division in the U.S., and I remember being excited by the fast-paced action that Tiger Mask demonstrated in that division. While overseas I was given a souvenir Tiger Mask mask to bring home to my sons. Joseph immediately adopted the mask is his matches against Gregory, who wrestled as Mil Máscaras. Through the years there have been five different wrestlers who have portrayed Tiger Mask, but the original, Satoru Sayama, is still the best.

"The Showstopper" and Diesel.

Can you smell what
the Rock is cooking?

No one in the WWF was ever quite like "Superstar" Billy Graham. Colorful, charismatic and with a look like no other, Superstar was the perfect man for his

time. I first met Superstar in 1974 in Houston, Texas. Afterwards I wrote several stories about him for *Wrestling Revue, Wrestling World, Wrestling News* and a few other publications, and every time a new article hit the newsstands he would call to thank me.

In 1975 Superstar called to tell me that he was going to be wrestling in the WWWF. I remember picking him up at the airport and taking him to my home for dinner before driving him to New York City to get a room for the night. We became close friends during that period, and I would often drive him to his bookings in New York, New Jersey and Connecticut. One Tuesday night in 1975 while Billy was at my home, I put on Championship Wrestling from Florida on UHF Channel 47. Billy pulled his chair up close to the small screen to get a better view as Dusty Rhodes came on. As Dusty went into his sing-song promo, Superstar blurted, "He stole my interview!" Billy hadn't seen Dusty in a few years, and when he heard him he was a little annoyed that he had "borrowed" his interview. Through the years Dusty wasn't the only one who "stole" from the Superstar. Graham always use to refer to his bulging biceps as his "24-inch pythons," and that's the same phrase that Hulk Hogan used to describe his arms almost 10 years later. Besides Hogan, Jesse "The Body" Ventura borrowed quite heavily from the Superstar as did a number of other stars from that era.

On April 30, 1977, during the Superstar's second stint in the WWWF, I drove him to Baltimore for his match against Bruno Sammartino. As we drove, Superstar said to me, "I hope you have a lot of film for my match tonight." I told him that I had enough photos of him versus Bruno, but he replied, "You're gonna need this for posterity." I still didn't catch on, and I was as surprised as everyone else when his arm was raised in victory and he was handed the WWWF world heavyweight championship title. Afterwards, a hush descended upon the crowd as Billy ran to the dressing room clutching the belt. I rushed to the dressing room to get a photo of the new champion with the belt but he said, "Let's go. We have to leave right away." Superstar was afraid he was going to have trouble leaving, with Sammartino fans out for revenge. Through the years our paths have crossed numerous times, and he has always been a true friend.

Sabu and Rob Van Dam land on Chris Candido and Lance Storm.

Terry Funk about to receive Sabu's right hand.

Ricky "The Dragon" Steamboat celebrates winning the title.

Ultimate Warrior clamps a bearhug on Hulk Hogan during their battle at *WrestleMania VI* at the SkyDome in Toronto, Canada, on April 1, 1990.

Sting attempts to finish Goldberg.

Snooki stands between the Rock and John Cena during their press conference at the Hard Rock Café in New York prior to *WrestleMania XXVII*.

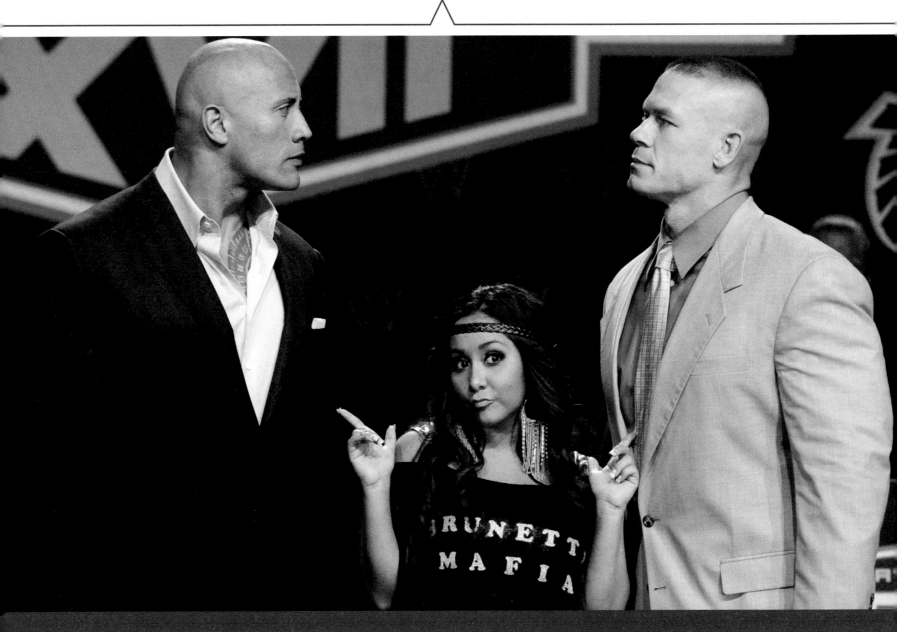

The Viper: Randy Orton.

It was 1978 when I was first introduced to a man who would revolutionize professional wrestling. I was standing in the dressing room area at the Philadelphia Arena when Fred Blassie came up to me and asked me to take photos of him and his new protégé. Blassie told me that the guy was green, but that he was going to be something someday. A few minutes later, the dressing room door opened and out stepped someone who dwarfed Blassie by several inches. I was then formally introduced to a man known as Hulk Hogan. He stood 6'7" and was very impressive. His chest hair was cut to resemble a tornado and his physique was incredible. I had never seen anyone as physically imposing as him. We took several photos with Blassie calling out the poses. You could sense that he was something special, but I had yet to see him in action. When he walked through the curtain you could hear the ooohs and aaaahs emanating from the crowd as Blassie lead him to the ring. Having Fred Blassie at his side was an indication to the fans that this youngster was going to be the next big thing, and he didn't disappoint, easily disposing of his opposition in mere seconds.

From our first introduction we became friends, and as time went on we would talk whenever we could. I vividly recall the night that Hulk Hogan wrestled Andre the Giant in Madison Square Garden in 1981. This was going to be one of Hogan's last matches before going to Hollywood to film *Rocky III*. The match was nothing special but during the bout Hogan's nose started to bleed. After the matches were over, I met Hogan at the Howard Johnson hotel at 49th Street and 8th Avenue. During dinner he asked if I saw what Andre did to him. I asked if he meant the bloody nose. He said yes, then proceeded to tell me that during the match Andre put up his fist and said, "Remember you're a wrestler not an actor," and then punched him in the nose, breaking it in three places. The next day Hogan was scheduled to go to Hollywood to film a screen test for *Rocky III* and he went with a broken nose compliments of Andre the Giant and the WWF. The powers that be in the WWF were not too pleased that one of their wrestlers was going to go to Hollywood to film a movie. At the time wrestlers were wrestlers and actors were actors, and those in the wrestling profession were very protective of their product and fearful of "outsiders." What a change from today when someone like Snooki can take part in *WrestleMania*, the biggest event of the year. After the Andre incident, Hogan wrestled several more matches in the WWF, then started in the AWA after *Rocky III* was released. However when Vince McMahon purchased controlling interest in the WWF from his father in 1982, he knew that he needed a marquee name to headline his new promotion and he approached Hulk Hogan about returning to the WWF. Needless to say Hulk did and the rest, as they say, is history.

Through the years Hulk Hogan has done it all. He's wrestled all over the world and brought as much success to WCW as he did to the WWF in those early years. Anyone who has any knowledge of the sport knows his history, and those who don't still know all about Hulk Hogan. He's an American icon.

"Thunderlips, baby."

"What'cha gonna do?"

Prior to the Japanese release of his record *Ichiban*, Hulk and I jammed together in a recording studio in Shinjuku.

When Hulk Hogan first started in the WWF, his manager was Fred Blassie. Mr. Vince McMahon Sr. wanted Fred Blassie's old school charm to rub off on the young Hogan, but the two never really hit it off.

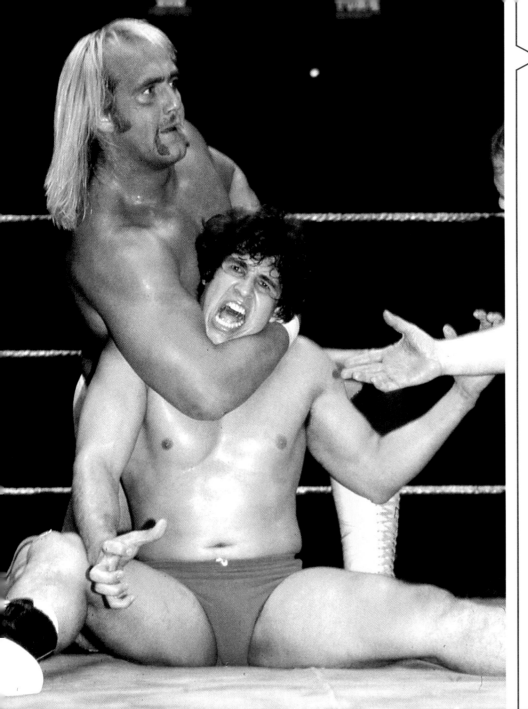

Hogan locks up Tito Santana.

Hollywood Hulk Hogan.

Mil Máscaras is holding Gregory while Jackie holds Joseph during one the grappler's many visits to my home. And yes, he took the mask off to eat. But if I showed a photo of him without his trademark mask, no one would know who it was.

My wife, Jackie, gets a lift from Andre before a 1974 match in Madison Square Garden.

Before a match in Brooklyn, New York, Abby has two new sidekicks hiding under his cape — my sons, Gregory and Joseph.

Of all the wrestlers I've seen through the years, "Stone Cold" Steve Austin ranks near the top of the list. The way he pumps up the crowd merely with his presence makes him one of the best wrestlers of any era.

"Classy" Freddie Blassie makes a pencil neck out of my son Gregory. Gregory was one of Fred Blassie's favorites, and he'd always ask me about him.

Champion Bob Backlund gives my son Gregory a lift during a backstage encounter in 1978 at a spot show in Brooklyn, New York. At that time the WWF held shows every week in small venues throughout the East Coast.

Luke Williams and Butch Miller indoctrinate their newest Bushwhacker, my son Joseph.

Road Warrior Hawk and Jim "The Anvil" Neidhart with my boys, Greg and Joe, before a spot show in Brooklyn, New York. Hawk would come by my house whenever he was in the neighborhood and you never knew who he was going to bring with him.

Bushwhacker Luke Williams (far left) along with Animal, who is holding Gregory, and Hawk, who has Joseph on his shoulders, visit the boys in the neighborhood outside Secrets during one of their many trips to Brooklyn.

Me and Máscaras.

Inside the dressing room area at the Philadelphia Arena, my son Joe flexes his muscles wearing the U.S. tag team title and decked out in Sting face paint as his partner "The Dog-Faced Gremlin" Rick Steiner looks on.

At a convention in Pennsylvania I was fortunate enough to renew acquaintances with old friends, Animal from the Road Warriors, Sid Vicious, the late Kerry Von Erich, Terry Funk and the late Nancy "Woman" Benoit.

Mr. Saito is training two karate kids: Gregory and Joseph.

Me with Hall of Famer Ric Flair in 1984 during the NWA convention in Puerto Rico. We had just traveled from Santo Domingo, where he had wrestled Jack Veneno in front of 20,000 rabid Dominica fans, and Ric couldn't find his passport to get back into Puerto Rico. In his haste to get out of Santo Domingo, he had left it in his hotel room, or so he thought. Luckily Carlos Colón had a friend in customs who cleared him.

Joe and Greg are mesmerized by Sgt. Slaughter and give the Sarge a salute in the dressing room at Wagner College in Staten Island.

Sting with my kids and their friends.

Superstar and my son.

My friend Andre the Giant and me. Dig those '70s duds!

I'm surrounded by two of my closest friends in the business — Ric Flair and Hulk Hogan — in 2010.

I was first introduced to Antonio Inoki in 1976, prior to his match with Muhammad Ali. In 1981 Inoki and his associate, WWWF President Hashi Shima, invited me to tour Japan with their New Japan Pro Wrestling organization. Through the years I was fortunate to visit Japan ten times.

After meeting Terra Ryzing, a.k.a. Triple H, in 1993 at a Connecticut spot show promoted by Killer Kowalski, I had my photo taken with this up-and-coming star.

Sting covers Hogan and the Disciple.

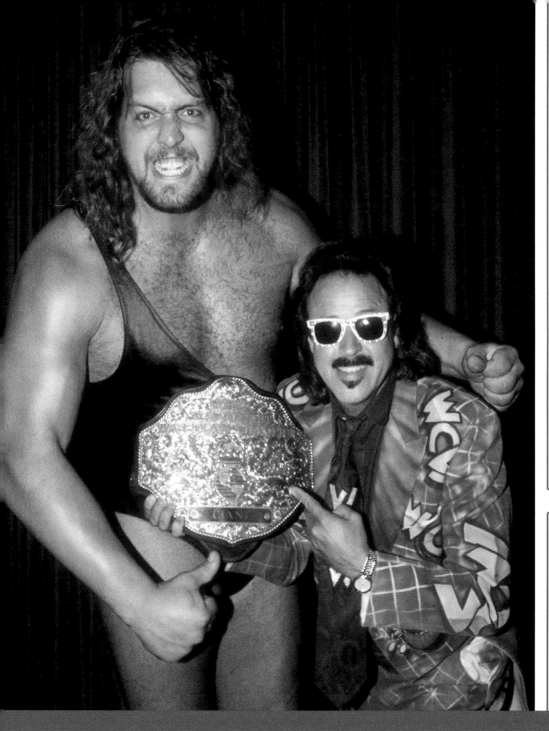

Before becoming a professional wrestler, Paul Wight, a.k.a. "The Big Show," came to a WCW match in Chicago and his chance meeting with Hulk Hogan and "The Mouth of the South" Jimmy Hart led to a professional career.

Bill Goldberg was at the height of his popularity in 1998 during the WCW Bash at the Beach.

Steve Austin, with his robe and flowing blond locks, strikes a pose wearing the U.S. title during his days in WCW.

Diamond Dallas Page makes an elaborate entrance to the ring during his WCW days. Back in the day the WCW ring entrances were even more stunning than those of the WWF.

Sid Vicious puts the boot to Bill Goldberg in their 1999 WCW match.

ECW champ Terry Funk.

Savage, DiBiase and Hogan in WCW.

Terry Funk is caught up in the barbed wire during one of his many wild bouts in Japan. I witnessed his badly battered and bruised body get stitched up time and time again after many of his WCW, ECW and Japanese bouts.

Diamond Dallas Page
and Karl Malone.

Hogan and Piper: a classic rivalry right to the end. Both men were there at the start during the WWF's rise and both are still two of the most charismatic men in the sport.

The Outsiders.

Scott Hall, Dennis Rodman, Hollywood Hogan, Macho Man and Syxx (kneeling) mug for the TV camera during a *Nitro* taping.

Buff Bagwell yells out in pain as Rick Steiner digs his fingers into his eye.

In 1998 Hulk Hogan enlisted the aid of basketball bad boy Dennis Rodman for a Bash at the Beach encounter with Diamond Dallas Page and Karl Malone.

In 1996 when it was announced that WCW was going to add a wrestling program on TNT, Sting, along with "Macho Man" Randy Savage and Hulk Hogan, appeared at the Harley-Davidson Café in New York City to break the news.

"The Bad Guy" Scott Hall had loads of talent and charisma.

"The best there is; the best there was; the best there will ever be."

Kevin Sullivan with Purple Haze, Bob Roop and the Acolytes: in the '80s Kevin Sullivan was the driving force behind Championship Wrestling from Florida. Although Dusty Rhodes was the big man in the promotion, it was Kevin Sullivan and his cast of characters that included Bob Roop, Purple Haze and the Fallen Angel who lit up Championship Wrestling from Florida.

In 1984 I was taking photos of wrestler Billy Jack, who readers of my *Wrestling All Stars* magazine voted "World's Sexiest Wrestler," and Kevin Sullivan happened to be in the adjoining dressing room watching what I was doing. Actually he was looking at one of the ladies that I posed with Billy Jack. She was a local girl named Nancy Daus, who actually sold the programs during the matches in Orlando. During the shoot Kevin, whom I had known since his WWWF days in the early '70s, came into the room and asked me who she was. I introduced him to Nancy, and during the course of the shoot he told her that he wanted to make her his valet. She just laughed it off, but Kevin was persistent. When the shoot was finished Kevin gave Nancy his number and told her that whenever she was ready, he wanted her to be his "Fallen Angel." Kevin looked for Nancy week after week whenever he went to Orlando and asked her the same question. Nancy, however, steadfastly refused until one day when she drove to Tampa, the home of Championship Wrestling from Florida, and told Kevin that she was ready to be his valet. Kevin immediately contacted Mike Graham and Dusty Rhodes and told them his plan. The "Fallen Angel" had descended to earth.

Kevin Sullivan and Fallen Angel.

> Terry Gordy, Buddy Roberts and Michael Hayes display their colors.

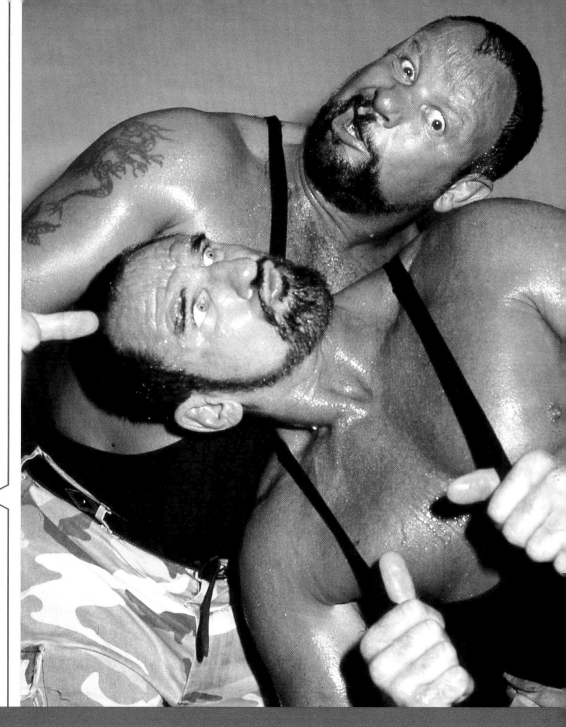

One of my all-time favorite tag teams and two of my closest friends, the Bushwhackers (a.k.a. the Sheepherders): Luke Williams and Butch Miller strike one of their classic poses.

The Ultimate Warrior in WCW.

> Moondog Spot, Captain Lou
Albano, Andy Kaufman and
Moondog Rex in the dress-
ing room at Madison Square
Garden.

The Iron Sheik swings his Persian clubs, which are used in an actual sport in his native Iran. An underappreciated fact: the Iron Sheik was an incredible wrestler in his day. He competed in the 1968 Olympics for Iran and later, after moving to the U.S., became the Assistant Coach for the U.S. Olympic wrestling team. He was trained professionally by Verne Gagne and was in the same wrestling class as Ric Flair. I first meet Khosrow Vaziri in 1974 in Houston, Texas. At the time he was no more than 200 pounds of rock solid muscle and was considered a "scientific" wrestler. We have remained friends ever since.

The Doink the Clown character was a far cry from the days of Bruno and Pedro, but it fit in perfectly with the WWF direction in the early '90s.

Jimmy "Superfly" Snuka wields a chair.

Justin Credible is about to dump Jerry Lynn to the mat.

In May 1998 Terry Funk was still going strong. Every month he would head to Philadelphia, Pennsylvania, to the ECW Arena to unleash his brand of mayhem on whomever he was matched against. This particular night manager Bill Alfonso was Funk's unfortunate victim.

Balls Mahoney prepares to punish Spike Dudley during their encounter in the ECW Arena in Philadelphia.

Bam Bam Bigelow puts Taz through a table during another one of their wild ECW bouts.

Sandman.

Manager Bill Alfonso inspects the barbed wire prior to a 1998 ECW match.

Bam Bam Bigelow flies through the air with Taz as his intended victim during a wild ECW bout in March 1998.

Rob Van Dam, the man who claims to be "The Whole F'N Show," has been a sensation wherever he has appeared.

They didn't come any more hardcore than the Dudleys during their ECW tenure. They epitomized what ECW was all about.

The men who made ECW hardcore: Devon, Dreamer and Bubba.

Chris Candido and Sabu go all out during a wild tables match in ECW.

Tommy Dreamer has Francine in a compromising position as he is about to deliver a pile driver during ECW action in Philadelphia.

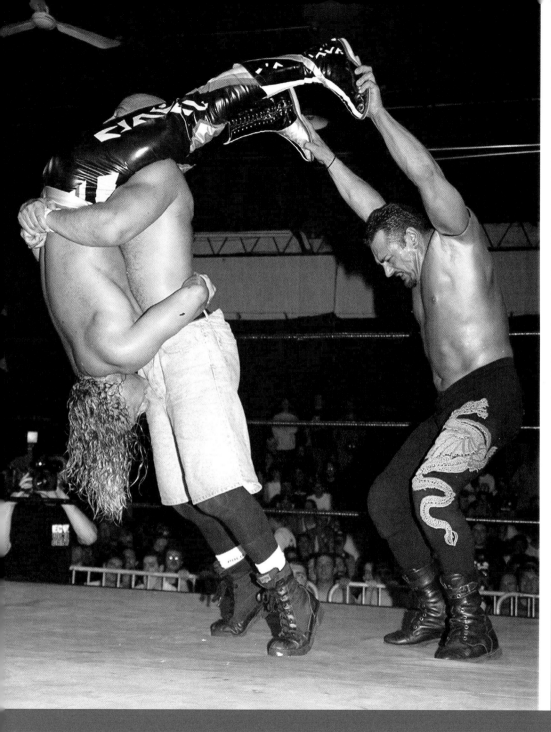

Jason Knight helps Justin Credible spike Jerry Lynn.

Terry Funk and
Sabu in ECW.

Sabu's death-defying aerial attack strikes Terry Funk.

Spike Dudley drop kicks Chastity in an ECW brawl.

Lance Storm soars above Sabu during one of their ECW brawls.

Sabu and ECW
super-pest Bill
Alfonso.

New Jack pounds Tracey Smothers with a guitar.

On the sign (shown upside down in image): ENTERING FORKS TOWNSHIP PEDDLERS MUST BE LICENSED

John Kronus of the Eliminators delivers a sidekick to Tracey Smothers.

Tommy Dreamer gets cozy with ECW ladies Kimona Wanalaya and Beulah McGillicutty. Dreamer later married Beulah and they have raised a beautiful family together.

While there are quite a few men who come to mind when you think of the heyday of ECW, no one epitomized ECW more than Sabu. He did it all and then some. His reckless, death-defying moves still send shivers up and down the spine of anyone who watched him during ECW's formative years. While you may be able to predict a pattern in many wrestlers' repertoires after watching them in the ring, you could never figure out what Sabu was going to do next. In fact, he never knew himself, and he would just do whatever came to mind at that particular moment. Photographing him was perhaps the hardest and most dangerous thing to do, but that's what made it exciting. Unfortunately Sabu paid the price for his reckless behavior inside the ring and never quite made it into the mainstream as so many others with lesser talent did. Despite this, the nephew of the original Sheik is still regarded as one of the wildest performers ever to step into the ring.

Sabu flies onto Tommy Dreamer while RVD pins the Hardcore original to a table.

RVD goes skyward and kicks a chair out of the hand of Jerry Lynn in classic ECW action.

Spike Dudley, the "runt" of the Dudley clan, made up for his lack of stature with pure heart and natural ability.

Shane Douglas slams Sabu in the heat of battle during one of their ECW encounters.

Sabu and Terry Funk.

The Dudley Boys, Sandman and ladders were just a few of the ingredients that made ECW so popular.

Taz was another of the big guns in ECW. He was known as "The Human Suplex Machine," and even men as big as Bam Bam Bigelow and Bubba Ray Dudley fell to his devastating power.

Touring Japan for New Japan Pro Wrestling was quite an experience. After one of the events all of the "foreigners" on the tour went to a restaurant to celebrate. My wife, Jackie (left), was also there as were Swede Hanson, Hulk Hogan, Andre the Giant, Wayne Bridges from England, Otto Wanz from Germany, Curt Hennig, Dick Murdoch and Adrian Adonis. That night Hogan said that he could eat more sushi than anyone on the tour, and they had an eating contest. They began to eat and Hulk was holding his own against Andre and Otto Wanz. Soon Andre and Otto began to put away food like there was no tomorrow. Seeing this, Hogan started grabbing the empty plates from Murdoch, Adonis, Hennig and myself, acting like he had eaten more than he had. When the time came to tally up the bill and see who ate more, Hogan had more plates in front of him. Andre then said, "Boss, since you ate the most, you have to pay the bill." Hogan forked over the money for the entire meal.

Stone Cold Steve Austin celebrates with Mike Tyson at *WrestleMania XIV*. This event brought the WWF back into prominence. Prior to *WrestleMania XIV*, WCW seemed to be winning the wrestling war, but with Austin, the Rock and the added appearance of Mike Tyson on the WWF telecasts, fans began to once again take an interest in the WWF.

Long Island native and New York Mets fan Cactus Jack pitches on the mound at the original home of the Mets, Shea Stadium, in September 2001.

Bubba, Devon and the hardcore Met mascot Mr. Met get together at Shea Stadium.

Owen Hart in 1997. Owen was my son Gregory's favorite wrestler. Owen would always take the time to talk with him whenever the opportunity arose.

Whenever he was in Brooklyn, Hawk would make it his business to spend time visiting with the neighborhood kids. Depending on the season he always attended my sons' football games, basketball games and baseball practices.

Triple H and his wife, Stephanie McMahon. If Vince ever decides to step away from the family business, he can rest easy knowing that the WWE is in the capable hands of his daughter, Stephanie, and son-in-law, Triple H.

I'm surrounded by two of my all-time favorites: Andre the Giant and Bruno Sammartino.

The "Macho Man"
Randy Savage and
his WCW valet
Gorgeous George.

"Captain" Lou Albano was as wild and crazy as anyone I ever met. When you talk about Hardcore, there really was no one crazier and wilder.

Sunny could be considered the first diva in the WWF. She came on the scene in the '90s and immediately made a huge impact, which earned her a spot in the WWE Hall of Fame in 2011.

The Undertaker has been a mainstay in the WWE since 1990. During his tenure he has done it all, and he could be the most revered wrestler in the company's history. I first met the Undertaker when he wrestled in WCW as one of the Skyscrapers, but I never imagined that he would evolve into such a storied character. When he finally calls it a career, the Undertaker could go down as the greatest WWE performer of all time.

Tajiri stands on the field at Shea Stadium wearing his New York Mets jersey.

"The Human Suplex Machine," Taz.

Stylin' and profilin' Ric Flair.

Hulk Hogan is all smiles as he holds up his cast jacket from *Rocky III*. This photo was taken in the Keio Plaza Hotel in Tokyo before *Rocky III* was released.

On tour in Japan in 1981 with Hulk Hogan, Curt Hennig (standing), Swede Hanson, Andre the Giant and England's Wayne Bridges (seated).

Psycho Sid Vicious slams the Dudley Boys during the
ECW Living Dangerously pay-per-view in 1999.

The Legion of Doom, Hawk and Animal, along with their manager "Precious" Paul Ellering, revolutionized the tag team wrestling scene. Individually either member could have been a champion on his own, but they made a conscious effort to stay together and establish their dominance in the tag team division. As a team the Road Warriors, as they were known in their AWA and WCW days, had few equals. From the moment their music hit and they barged through the dressing room doors, the fans knew they were in for a treat. While there were a few other good tag teams during the Road Warriors' heyday, Hawk and Animal were simply in a class by themselves. Of all the wrestlers I've had the privilege of knowing in my 40-plus years covering the sport, they were my closest friends. I can't begin to count the number of times that Hawk and Animal would make a side trip to Brooklyn to hang out and get away from the hectic grind of traveling from city to city. My wife would cook for them and my son Gregory at eight years old would eat as much as them. They attended baseball, basketball and football games. They ate at Gargiulo's in Brooklyn, and in fact we even had a special wedding party at Gargiulo's for Hawk and his wife, Dale. Then there was the night when some wise guys were hassling the owner of Gargiulo's, Louie. Louie mentioned to Hawk a problem that he was having in the catering hall and Hawk, along with Dustin Rhodes, straightened out the situation. One day before a match in Madison Square Garden, Hawk even showed up at my wife's school, PS 229, to talk to her fourth grade class. While the Road Warriors are no more, their legacy will live on in the hearts of everyone they came in contact with in their storied career.

Devon and Bubba perform their 3D signature move on brother Spike during a match in 1999.

Bushwhacker Luke Williams and Johnny Ace visit New York City nightclub Shout in 1984. Whenever the boys came to New York they always wanted to go out after the matches. Invariably we would wind up at either John's Pizzeria of Bleecker Street or the Carnegie Deli, and then make the rounds visiting the Cat Club, the China Club or whatever new hot spot my friend Lonnie Hanover was promoting.

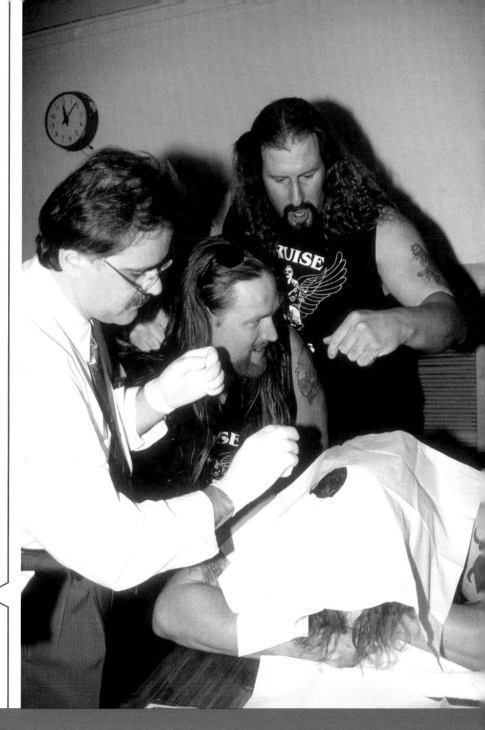

The Harris Twins "help" provide medical assistance after a gruesome battle in Philadelphia.

Luke and Butch of the Bushwhackers back in the days when they were known as the Sheepherders. Standing behind them is their ring bearer Johnny "Ace" Laurinaitis, who today is Executive Vice-President of Talent Relations for the WWF.

Missy Hyatt, captured in the days of the UWF, in a classic pose with Hot Stuff International. Pictured are Sting, Jack Victory, Missy, "Hollywood" John Tatum, Eddie Gilbert and Rick Steiner. A short while later Jim Crockett bought the UWF from Bill Watts and merged it into WCW.

The Legion of Doom.

Dennis Condrey of the Midnight Express and Road Warrior Hawk hang off a scaffold during their match at the Omni on November 27, 1986, during Starrcade.

Shawn Michaels was another wrestler I watched with interest as he grew into superstardom. While he was not the biggest wrestler in the business by far, Shawn Michaels exhibited more heart, guts, fire and determination than any wrestler I have ever seen. Whether it was as part of the Midnight Rockers with Marty Jannetty, in his "Sexy Boy" days with Sensational Sherri, in his superb series of bouts against Razor Ramon with Diesel by his

side, or as a member of DX with his close friend Triple H, Shawn Michaels was always on top of his game. Shawn Michaels' career is like a highlight reel with each different "era" a different chapter in the life and times of one of the most charismatic wrestlers that I have seen in my 40 years covering the sport.

During the '80s the Fabulous Ones (Stan Lane and Steve Keirn), Austin Idol and "The Boogie Woogie Man" Jimmy Valiant were huge favorites in the NWA.

The Midnight Express — Jim Cornette flanked by Dennis Condrey and Bobby Eaton — was another great tag team combination in the '80s. While I didn't know Jim Cornette personally as his career began, we both worked for *Wrestling News* magazine. Throughout the '70s Cornette covered the Memphis scene for *Wrestling News*, while I did the same for the WWWF.

While the Road Warriors may have been the most devastating tag team in the sport in the '80s, the Rock 'n' Roll Express, consisting of Robert Gibson and Ricky Morton, was still the most popular. Individually neither member was big or powerful, but together they had few equals in the ring.

The nWo with Syxx, Scott Hall and Kevin Nash controlled not only the tag team scene but also the entire WCW.

Ink Inc.: Shannon Moore and Jesse Neal double team Devon Dudley.

Mick Foley trashes Abdullah the Butcher
during a brawl in Atlanta, Georgia.

Cactus Jack and W*ING Kanemura go all out in their barbed wire

barricade spider net glass crush death match in Japan.

What a storied career the legendary Terry Funk has had. From becoming NWA World Heavyweight Champion in 1975 by defeating Jack Brisco, to taking the ECW Hardcore title, Terry Funk has done it all. He started his career in Texas under the guidance of his father, Dory Funk Sr., and traveled all around the world winning titles everywhere he ever appeared. In addition to being an outstanding singles wrestler, Terry also teamed with his brother Dory Jr. to make one of the most successful tag teams in the country. Terry, who was schooled in the old style of '60s wrestling, somehow was able to effortlessly make the transition to the wild ECW style. Often after seeing his battered and tattered body following a grueling ECW battle, I'd ask Terry how he was able to do what he did. He would just shrug and say with a smile, "I have no idea!" I also remember Terry admonishing me one time in 1990 after he saw that I placed him in the "All Time Greats" section of my book *The New Pictorial History of Wrestling* alongside such legends as Andre the Giant, Bruiser Brody, Lou Thesz and Buddy Rogers. He looked me straight in the eye and blurted, "Do I look f'n dead to you?!" Then he smiled that crooked smile of his, pulled me to him and gave me a hug. That's typical Terry Funk.

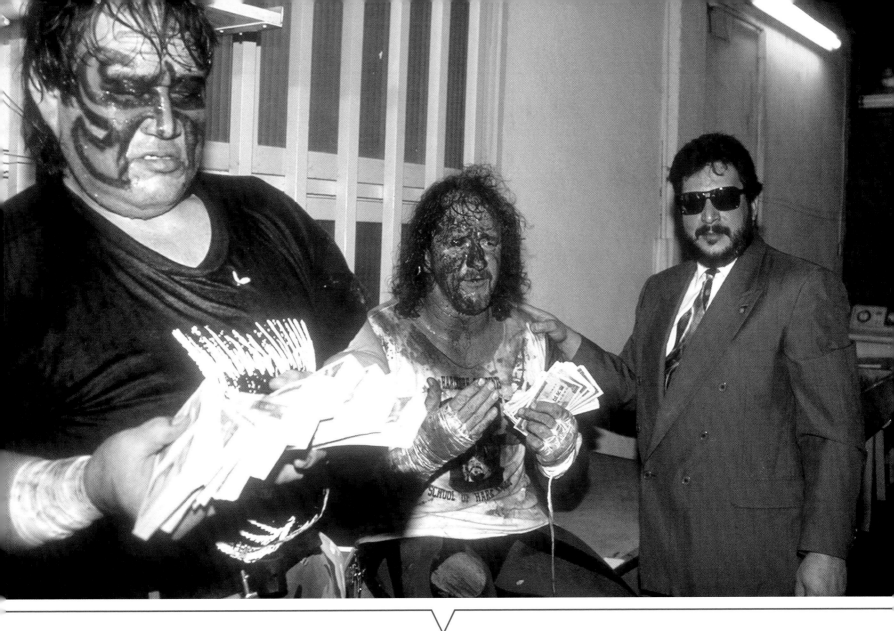

Mr. Pogo and Terry Funk along with their manager and my good friend,
the late Victor Quiñones, after their legendary FMW bout in Japan.

Cactus Jack wields a barbed-wire bat during his wild brawl with Triple H.

"The American Dream" Dusty Rhodes has Tully Blanchard tied up in their 1986 Texas bullrope match in Greensboro.

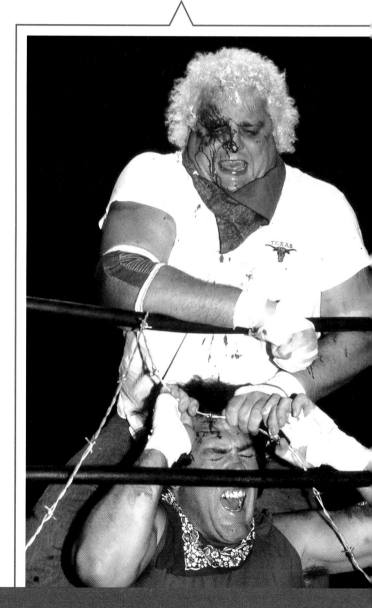

Hardcore was the way Bubba Ray and Devon earned their name and reputation.

The original Hardcore legends Abdullah the Butcher and Bruiser Brody go at it in a wild bout in San Juan, Puerto Rico.

Megumi Kudo is a battered mess after her 1996 blood curdling FMW no rope electrified explosive barbed wire death match with Combat Toyoda. Onita and Hayabusa, who came into the dressing room to check on the fallen Kudo, are stunned by the extent of her burns as they are swarmed by Japanese photographers and media. Out of the thousands and thousands of matches I have seen and photographed, this bout ranks near the top as one of the wildest I have ever witnessed.

Cactus Jack, a.k.a. Mick Foley, worked very hard to make it in the profession. He started out by setting up rings for the local shows in Brooklyn, New York, and made it all the way to headlining shows in Madison Square Garden. Along the way he became a true Hardcore icon and reinvented himself numerous times to stay on top of his game.

Cactus Jack wreaks havoc in Japan during a vicious barbed wire battle.

ECW had some wild characters, and the Sandman was right near the top of the list. The chain-smoking, cane-swinging, beer-drinking Sandman was as tough as nails. He took a beating but kept on ticking night after night after night.

Terry Funk gives Sabu a lift.

Jeff Hardy power-bombs Abyss onto the tacks in a Brooklyn Hardcore battle.

Mr. Anderson, as he is known in TNA, jumps off the top rope onto Jeff Hardy in TNA action in 2010 at the Manhattan Center in New York City.

Tommy Dreamer introduces TNA's Abyss to a Hardcore staple: a trashcan to the face.

TNA's Abyss rearranges Tommy Dreamer's face during their New York brawl in 2010.

Hardcore icon Tommy F'N Dreamer lets out a scream after his TNA victory in New York City.

Kurt Angle tosses Desmond Wolfe around the ring during their battle in Brooklyn's MCU Park in summer 2010.

The ankle lock does it for Kurt Angle as he makes Desmond Wolfe submit in their summer 2010 battle in Brooklyn.

Rob Van Dam's boot connects with A.J. Styles's face in Brooklyn.

Many wrestling aficionados feel that "The Phenomenal" A.J. Styles could be the new face of the sport.

Terry Funk and Mr. Pogo blow a double fireball, which burns Hayabusa's back during the main event in their no rope exploding barbed wire double hell landmine time bomb match at Kawasaki Baseball Stadium on May 5, 1996.

"Captain" Lou Albano, "The Grand Wizard of Wrestling" Ernie Roth and "Classy" Freddie Blassie were the men who made it possible for me to do what I have done for all these years. During the '70s and early '80s, I would drive all three managers to Madison Square Garden along with whoever was in the main event that night facing Bruno Sammartino or Pedro Morales or Bob Backlund. Those car rides from the Howard Johnson Hotel on 49th Street to MSG were sometimes wilder than the matches!

Larry Zbyszko, a Pittsburgh native like Bruno, was the only wrestler than Bruno personally trained and brought into the business. Zbyszko later tried to capitalize on this by calling himself "The Living Legend." Incidentally Bruno was my favorite wrestler while growing up. In fact I was in Madison Square Garden on May 17, 1963, sitting in the blue seats when he defeated Buddy Rogers to win the WWWF world title. What a thrill it was for me when I finally met my child-hood hero face to face in Sunnyside Gardens after being introduced to him by his manager Arnold Skaaland.

Bruiser Brody could have been the greatest brawler of all time, but unfortunately his life was cut short when he was stabbed in a dressing room after a match in San Juan, Puerto Rico.

Missy Hyatt gets down and dirty in Texas Stadium.

At the County Center in White Plains, New York, I managed to get international superstars Mil Máscaras, Andre the Giant and "The American Dream" Dusty Rhodes to pose together for a photo. Considering their schedules, seeing all three of these wrestlers on the same bill in White Plains was truly astonishing.

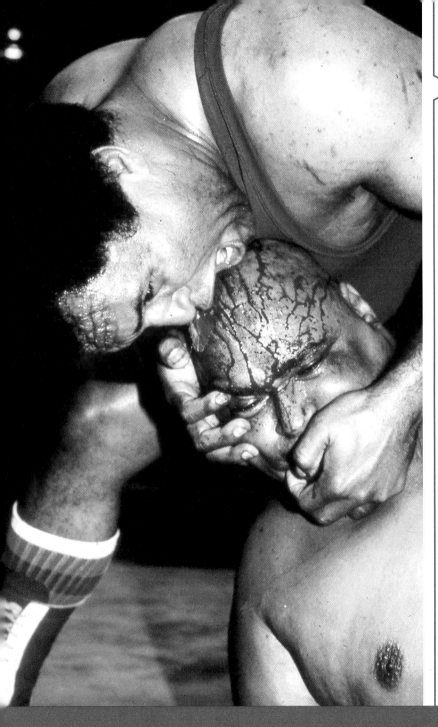

Carlos Colón takes a bite out of the Butcher during one of their numerous battles in Puerto Rico.

It was quite a stretch
to see former NWA
World Heavyweight
Champions Dory
Funk Jr. and Terry
Funk compete in
ECW. In the '70s they
were considered two
of the greatest pure
wrestlers, and then,
nearly 20 years later,
both were spilling
their blood and guts
in ECW rings.

Cactus Jack, as "Mankind," smelling the flowers while we were on tour in Japan for FMW in 1997.

WWF champion Bob Backlund tosses NWA champion "Nature Boy" Ric Flair during a double title match in St. Louis, Missouri. At this time it was very rare to see a WWF wrestler on the same bill with an NWA wrestler, let alone a match with both titles on the line.

Classic Macho Man.

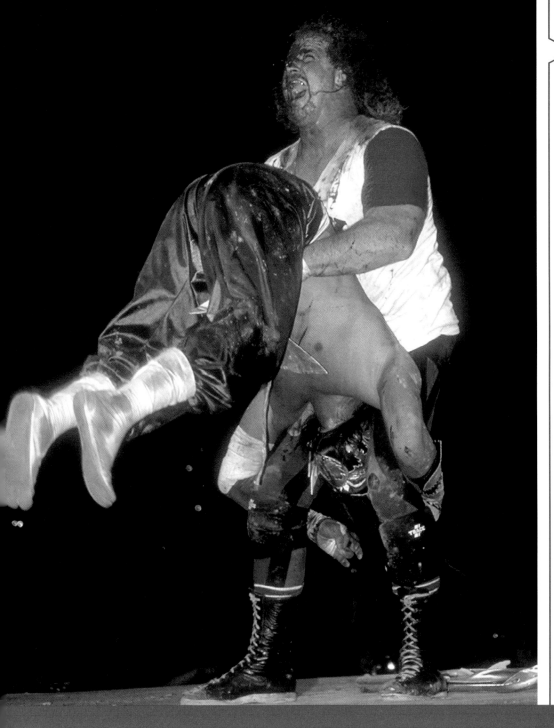

FMW 1996: Terry Funk
lifts Hayabusa.

Mr. Pogo and Hayabusa.

In May 1996 I was invited to Japan to photograph the FMW tour featuring Cactus Jack and Terry Funk. This turned out to be the wildest, craziest and most dangerous set of matches that I've ever witnessed. Terry Funk and Mr. Pogo faced Masato Tanaka and Hayabusa in a no rope exploding barbed wire double hell landmine time bomb match in the main event at Kawasaki Stadium on May 5, 1996. Towards the finish, Mr. Pogo poured lighter fluid on Masato Tanaka and then threw a fireball at him. I was right there and felt the heat as the flames erupted. When the bout was over Terry Funk spent the night in hospital recovering from third-degree burns.

At the end of the bout Terry Funk, along with Mr. Pogo and Victor Quiñones, taunted the crowd.

Kerry Von Erich defeats Ric Flair on May 6, 1984, in Texas Stadium in front of 45,000 to capture the NWA world heavyweight title. Kerry's victory was dedicated to his brother David, who had died three months earlier.

Ric Flair and Harley Race battle during their wild 1983 Starrcade match in Greensboro.

Woman, Nature Boy and Miss Elizabeth during one of Flair's many reigns.

The Hitman.

Superstar Billy Graham was on top of the world in 1977. This photo was taken in Graham's house in Long Beach, New York, on May 1, the day after the Superstar won the WWF worlds title from Bruno Sammartino in Baltimore.

The Von Erich family: Fritz, Mike, Kevin, Chris and Kerry get together after the David Von Erich Memorial Heaven Needed a Champion card in Texas Stadium in 1984.

Road Warrior Hawk was one of my closest friends in the business. We spent many days together on the road and in New York during his numerous trips to the city.

Nick Bockwinkel was an excellent scientific wrestler. He was a four-time AWA World Champion and, along with his partner Ray Stevens and manager Bobby "The Brain" Heenan, held the AWA Tag Team Title on three occasions. Today Bockwinkel lives in Las Vegas and is president of the Cauliflower Alley Club.

Hall of Fame members Johnny Rodz, Jimmy Snuka and Captain Lou get together before a TV taping in Hamburg, Pennsylvania.

Jerry Lawler gets hardcore ECW-style with Tommy Dreamer during their wild battle at Hardcore Heaven in 1997.

Shawn Michaels,
Chyna and Triple H.

Lex Luger had the look that everyone envied. In fact, one of my photos of Lex Luger was used in the opening scenes of *The Wrestler*. The movie opens inside a trailer with the camera panning to an old photo of a young and well-built Mickey Rourke, a.k.a. Randy "The Ram" Robinson. However, while the photo did have Mickey Rourke's face, it was superimposed onto a Lex Luger photo from his WCW days.

Pat Patterson in Japan.

Cowboy Bob "Ace" Orton stands behind "Rowdy" Roddy Piper during their time together during the first *Wrestle-Mania*. These days "Cowboy" Bob is better known as the father of one of today's top WWE superstars, Randy Orton.

Roddy Piper introduces Hulk Hogan to a steel cage.

The people's champ.

Before the current crop of WWE divas made the scene, Sable was *the* WWE sex symbol.

Randy Savage
tosses Ric Flair.

Superfly batters Bob Backlund.

Throughout the Mid-Atlantic Championship wrestling and WCW days of the '80s, there wasn't a more popular wrestler than Sting. He was by far the most charismatic wrestler in the promotion. While other men may have held the titles, Sting was the man that everyone came out to see, and you never left disappointed. During the '90s he reinvented himself somewhat, changing his classic look with white face paint, but for Sting the results were still the same.

George "The Animal" Steele.

The pedigree.

Kevin Sullivan and Bob Roop.

Taz, "The Human Suplex Machine," perfectly executes his finishing move on Vito "The Skull" LoGrasso of the Baldies.

Superstar Billy Graham in a MSG bullrope match with Dusty Rhodes.

In 1998 the Ultimate Warrior entered WCW and confronted his old nemesis Hulk Hogan.

ACKNOWLEDGMENTS

This book would not have been possible without the help and cooperation of Vince McMahon and his family, the thousands of wrestling stars I have had the pleasure of coming into contact with over the years, and the millions and millions of fans worldwide who follow the wild and wacky world of professional wrestling.